PRAYING
with Icons

Linette Martin

PARACLETE PRESS
BREWSTER, MASSACHUSETTS

Praying with Icons

2011 First Printing

Copyright © 2011 by Joe Walton Martin

ISBN: 978-1-61261-058-0 (Pack of Five)

The Library of Congress has catalogued the original book *Sacred Doorways*, from which this book is excerpted, as follows:

Martin, Linette.
  Sacred doorways : a beginner's guide to icons / Linette Martin.
    p. cm.
  Includes bibliographical references.
  ISBN 1-55725-307-2
  1. Icons—History. 2. Icon painting—Themes, motives. 3. Christianity and art—Orthodox Eastern Church. 4. Christian art and symbolism. I. Title.
  N8187.M37 2002
  704.9′482—dc21
                                            2002011555

10 9 8 7 6 5 4 3 2 1

Published by Paraclete Press
Brewster, Massachusetts
www.paracletepress.com

Printed in the United States of America

CONTENTS

ONE
What Are Icons?

COMPUTERS HAVE ICONS. Each one is a
simple sign with a specific meaning that evokes a
response. There is one that means "wastebasket,"
another "page," another "document." When we
know what each one is (most are easy enough to
recognize), we know what to do with it. The icon
points us to something beyond itself. Highways
have icons. They are signs simple enough to
recognize at speed, like "humpback bridge" or
"double hairpin bend." When we recognize the
sign, we do something, or if we are bad drivers we
do nothing.

A religious icon is the same as a computer icon
and a highway sign. It is graphic art: information
concentrated in visual iconography. A Christian of
the Orthodox Church would protest that a holy
icon is far more; as a Western Christian I would
say it is not less. The icon points us to something
beyond itself; we recognize it and are expected to
respond. That response may be belief, or disbelief,
or praise, or wonder, or prayer, or encouragement,
or terror about the Last Judgment or questions
about Christian doctrine. The icon insists that
we respond as much with the mind as with the

emotions. Icons are not directed only to the gut;
they are the thinking man's art.

That is what makes an icon different in motive
and in effect from some other religious pictures,
and that is why some people dislike icons: they
prefer Christian art to be decorative and unde-
manding. The Orthodox Church teaches that an
icon is a two-way door of communication that not
only shows us a person or an event but makes it
present. When we stand in front of an icon we are
in touch with that person and we take part in that
event. The historical event of the Nativity is here
and now to us, when we look at a *Nativity* icon.
What we call "our world" and what we call "the
spiritual world" are opened to each other.

According to the ancient teaching of the early
church and today's Eastern Orthodox Church, an
icon is a door. If you cannot believe that it is a
door, never mind. For you, I hope that icons come
to be seen as beautiful and rich pictures, showing
God and his work in a visual language that can be
understood.

ANY MATERIALS, ANY SIZE AND NOT ONLY RELIGIOUS

Today, we think icons portray only religious
subjects, but one and a half thousand years ago the
subject was not always religious. If a picture was of
an emperor or an important official, the craftsman
who made it would call it an icon, and in that broad

definition (icon = image) he was right. The picture of the emperor announced that the authority of the emperor was present. A national icon in the present day from any monarchy in the world is the picture of the monarch on a postage stamp.

In the New Testament, the Greek word εἰκων is translated "image," "likeness," "portrait." The Old and New Testaments use a word for "image" to describe all of us being in the image of the God who made us (Gen. 1:26; Matt. 22:20; Col. 1:15). In that sense an icon has written this book and an icon is now reading it. There is a Jewish saying that thousands of angels go before every human being, crying, "Make way, make way for the image of God."

A religious icon can be of Christ, the Virgin Mary, an angel, or a saint; it can be of an event from the Old or New Testament, or of a saint's life. It is painted on a wooden panel that is small enough to be portable, and placed on a shelf in someone's home for domestic devotion. Icons like that were made by the thousand and were an enriching focus of devotion for countless thousands of Christians, from famous theologians to the so-called "simple faithful." Icons were not only painted on a wooden panel. They were also made in mosaic, textile, enamel, fresco, ceramic, ivory or bone, silver or gold, bronze, and various semiprecious stones. They could be large and built into a wall-to-wall icon screen across the inside of an Orthodox Church or they could be as small as 2 inches (5 cm.) square and hung around someone's neck.

The size made no difference and the materials made no difference. They were all icons as long as they were made in the canonical visual language of the Eastern Orthodox Church.

The visual language is not changeless and rigid, as though someone decided, a thousand years ago, that a picture of Christ or the Virgin should be done according to a precise recipe that generations of craftsmen just followed without thinking. The visual language of icons has developed over centuries because it is a language. Just as a spoken language develops but remains itself, so does that of icons. Most people in Britain and the United States speak English. Though it is not exactly like the English spoken by Geoffrey Chaucer in the fourteenth century, it is recognizably the same language. It has developed but it is still English, and with a little help, modern English speakers can learn to read Chaucer. In the same way, the visual language of icons has developed over one and a half thousand years (and still is developing), but it is still recognizably itself. With only a little help Western people can learn to read it. The word for visual language is *iconography*. To an art historian an icon is a picture made in the visual language, the iconography, of the Orthodox Church.

To an Orthodox Christian a holy icon is a picture that is made according to the iconography of the Orthodox Church and that has been blessed by an Orthodox priest with the proper prayers. When you see a picture in an art gallery, can you tell? Perhaps. A picture that has been blessed does not glow with holy light; its status is hidden. Orthodox Christians will tell you that a holy icon is a picture made by a believing craftsman. When you see a picture in a gallery, can you tell? Of course not. There have been thousands of craftsmen working in and beyond the Byzantine Empire since the fourth century. If their personal faith flickered low they could still have followed the proper iconography and produced good, or at least adequate, work. On the other hand, an icon infused with prayer will have an indefinable "plus" quality that may come across even to a not particularly spiritual beholder.

TWO
Their Brief History

A USEFUL STARTING DATE TO REMEMBER is AD 330. That was when the Roman Emperor Constantine moved his court from Rome to a fishing town on the shores of the Black Sea. The little town had been there since the seventh century BC and was called *Byzantion*. The Emperor enlarged it to be a suitably imperial city and renamed it New Rome. Then it was named after him, Constantinople.

At its greatest extent, the Byzantine Empire stretched from the Alps to North Africa and from East of the Black Sea to the Spanish Peninsula. Over the centuries its fortunes and boundaries ebbed and flowed. It was captured by Turks in 1453 and renamed *Constantiniya*. It was not until the twentieth century, with the modernization by Kamil Ataturk, that the Turks took the Greek words *eis ten polin*, meaning "toward the town" and bent them into the name "Istanbul." From the date 1453, hear in your mind's ear the cry of a muezzin from a minaret, *"Alla.a.a..bbb akb-ba.a.a.r. . . ."* Constantinople had become what it is today: a Muslim town between Europe and the Middle East.

The visual language—the iconography—of icons, began to develop even before Constantine and was established in the Byzantine Empire between 330 and 1453, the period of time that historians call Late Antique and Medieval. After 1453, it was affected by the Western Renaissance to some extent, but its special qualities survived. In the West, icons were largely unappreciated during the twentieth century. In the mid-nineteenth century Byzantine items owned by the British Museum were stowed away in the basement with folk artifacts from Peru and Mexico. As recently as the 1920s a writer dismissed "Byzantine Madonnas and saints, conventionally featured, conventionally clad, conventionally colored, which are so definitely characteristic of western art in its cradle." Now people are discovering that Orthodox Christian art is not an outdated style whose only purpose was to inspire Duccio, but is something beautiful in its own right. There was no precise date when the visual language began because it grew out of Roman art; there was no date when it ended because it is still a living art.

When Were Icons First Made?

The earliest surviving icons are to be dated to the sixth and seventh centuries, and are almost all now preserved in the monastery of St. Catherine of Sinai. The remoteness of this outpost of the Empire preserved them from the systematic destruction of sacred art ordered by the iconoclast emperors after 720. All are in a technique and medium called "encaustic wax," in which powdered mineral colors were blended in hot wax, laid on with glass rods. By the time of the restoration of the icons in 843, this technique had been lost, and we are only now beginning to learn some idea of how it was done.

However, literary sources make it clear that icons were being made from the late fourth century. For example, St. John Chrysostom speaks of having a portrait of St. Paul on his desk to inspire him when writing homilies on the Epistles. Already at that time, there were a small minority of Churchmen (e.g., Eusebius of Caesarea, Epiphanius of Salamis) who had reservations concerning the legitimacy of images. Antipathy to Christian art did not begin with iconoclasm, though the fact that there was no controversy till the eighth century shows that the overwhelming majority of believers had no objections. By the late sixth century, indeed, icons were the principal focus of popular devotion among all classes throughout the eastern Roman world.

THREE

Getting Started

Icons, in the orthodox tradition, are made by praying artists for the distinct purpose of prayer. They are considered windows to spiritual truth.

The icon acts as a two-way channel: It communicates to the worshiper something of the presence and grace of the one depicted, and conveys to the sacred person the "prayer of the mind."

What makes it an icon is its special iconography and theological aesthetic, a way of presenting the great people and events of Christianity that is above art fashion and is therefore never going to look out of date. It is not meant to be a realistic picture like something seen through a camera lens, because it is more important than that; it shows the spiritual reality as well as the outer aspect. Some icons have several events of Old or New Testament history in one picture, because the whole event is important; some dispense with background and show a saint standing on tiptoe against a sheet of gold, because he is living in the light of God. Icons should never show God except as Incarnate Son. In prayer and stillness before icons we see this incarnational light.

FIRST THINGS FIRST: LOOK AT ICONS IN SILENCE AND STILLNESS

The first response to an icon should be silence. Later there can be time to analyze the details, admire the composition, or try to work out what pigments the craftsman used. First it is best to look in silence and let the icon say something to you. Look at the faces, then at the hands. Read the inscriptions if you can, but look longest at the faces and the hands. The first meeting with an icon is similar to a first meeting with a cat: approach with courtesy, and let the cat open the conversation.

In their stillness icons call into question our self-important bustle, our inner lack of integration and central calm. What the American writer Tom Howard has written about structured prayers applies to the formal dignity of these images:

> One does not bustle into the Divine Presence with a frantic agenda of personal concerns. One takes one's place with the morning stars who sang together, with the archangelical host of heaven, and with all the company of the faithful, doing the thing that Adam was placed in the garden in order to do, namely, to bless God.[1]

The sheer horizons of one's imagination are enlarged.

What I love about icons is that they do not allow us to bustle. They quieten us. They enlarge us. Even though some of the figures are painted as in movement, icons have a quality of stillness. They invite a quiet looking, and people who walk around an icon exhibition, where they can see a lot of icons close-up, feel that stillness.

The famous Novgorod icon of *St. George* shows him in the act of pig-sticking the dragon. The saint is mounted on a leaping horse, and the dragon's long tail coils in death, but in spite of the action there is a stillness. There is no third dimension in the picture space: The horse is painted without modeling; there is only a flat, horse-shaped white area silhouetted against a red sky. St. George's pencil-thin lance is unrealistically long and he is poised on the horse as though he had no weight. Both saint and horse have an expression of compassion. It is possible to look at that icon for some time without feeling restless. A distinguished Russian theologian observes:

> The saints are shown in stillness because they are becalmed in God; their eyes are open because they are keenly and prayerfully aware of our world. The less the body moves, the better do we perceive the movement of the spirit, for the corporeal world becomes its transparent shell. By expressing spiritual life with nothing but the eyes of a perfectly motionless figure, the artist symbolically conveys the immense power of the spirit over the flesh. One gets the impression that all corporeal life is stilled,

waiting for the highest revelation, listening for it. (E.N. Trubetskoi)

The search for holy stillness has always existed in the Christian Church. One place for a Westerner to discover it is in icons.

ARRESTED MOVEMENT

Looking at the *Pantocrator*, we are confronted with the changeless reality of Christ as Judge and Savior, or the *Virgin and Child* as presenting the fact of the Incarnation; looking at an icon of the *Raising of Lazarus*, we see the same Jesus Christ acting in a moment of human, historical time, but yet also a moment of eternal significance.

If we had been there with a camera, the figures might have been arranged differently showing the moment in arrested movement, a decisive moment of time when the clock ticked and something unrepeatable happened. But iconography makes it possible to show a moment of history, and to point to its spiritual significance. It shows us timelessness in time.

There are many other examples of arrested movement in icons. Elijah is swept up to heaven in a fiery chariot, his cloak drops to the ground toward his successor, Elisha. The archangel runs in to tell the Virgin Mary that she has been chosen to bear the Messiah. The archangel's wings are half spread and his feet barely touch the floor. At her surprise, the spindle in her hand drops. In a *Dormition* icon Christ lifts up the Virgin Mary's soul and holds her for us all to see: death is not a process but a decisive moment of time, shown by the swinging of the censer. In an Early Byzantine *Annunciation* mosaic (St. Maria Maggiore, Rome, fifth century), an archangel stands, and turns, and turns again from facing the Virgin to facing St. Joseph. As we run our eyes over the picture from left to right, we almost have the experience of watching a figure in movement. A hagiographical icon has the saint in the center, confronting us in great stillness, while the surrounding pictures show him in moments of arrested movement.

SILENT PRAYER

Silence is a form of prayer. But it leads naturally to other forms of prayer. Don't be overwhelmed by praying with icons. Think about simply growing toward prayer from that place of silence to a new place, as gently and naturally as the growing of a plant.

This is one place we learn to know God. We come to know God in the same ways we learn to know another human being. When you stop to think about it, how else could we know the Incarnate Christ? We look and we like what we see; we spend more time together in speech and in silence; we meet one another's friends and find interests in common. If anything has been written, we read it with attention; we share experiences, good and bad; we listen to what mutual friends say and watch how our new acquaintance speaks and acts with someone else. We grow closer to that person, unconsciously reproducing in ourselves what we see as the best in them. Slowly we become more involved in the relationship until we commit ourselves to the one we have learned to love. And it is this communion that is essential:

> The icon . . . fills a constant task, which has been that of Christian art from the beginning: to reveal the true relationships between God and man. . . . To the disoriented world the icon brings a testimony of authenticity, of the reality of another way of life. . . . The icon [can teach us] about God, man, and creation, a new attitude toward the world. (Leonid Ouspensky, *Theology of the Icon*)

VENERATION AS PRAYER

When we meet God through the veneration of an icon, that is, through prayer, he sees to it that we meet ourselves. For many people it is hard to know which confrontation is the more unnerving. This stillness of looking at an icon can turn into prayer, and into understanding, sometimes into confrontation.

> People outside the Christian world think that prayer is an occupation suited to the old and the sick, a harmless pastime like eating baby

food and being wrapped in a shawl. In fact, we see when icons confront us in our silence that there is a more bracing world out there, a great, wild, rich landscape that saints and mystics have explored. Some of them have sent messages back to base, describing the terrain, warning of dangers, and mapping some of the paths. We see those messages outlined here with icons. Those who pray must be deeply engaged with the spiritual realism the icon offers them; if not, they will never approach its mystery and it will for them only be a design without a soul. And for the one to whom it is given to contemplate God in the holy icon, it becomes an unerring path toward a transfiguration in Christ. (Georg Wunderle, *Um die Seele der heiligen Ikone*)

A WAY TO PRAY IN COLOR

Often a color in an icon does not mean anything: It simply balances the colors in the rest of the picture. For example, the icon of *St .George and the Dragon* painted in Novgorod is almost all in red, white, and steely blues. Beneath the saddle there is a quilted cloth painted in shades of tawny yellow. When we cover that part of the picture, the other colors go a little flat without the small contrast. It does not dominate the icon, but without it something is lost.

Much symbolism of color is obvious. Red, the color of blood, turns the mind to thoughts of life and vibrancy, or in the case of a martyr, death.

Less obvious to modern Western eyes is that deep, reddish-brown purple was the highest color in the spectrum in alchemy. It had connotations of sacred monarchy, so it was worn by the Virgin Mary and by emperors. Yellow is the color of the sun and of life. The background of a saint may be gold or yellow to show that the saint is living in eternal light. Angel faces in Western art are the color of Caucasian flesh; faces of icon angels are sometimes golden as though glowing with the light of God.

Green, the color of leaves in springtime, speaks naturally of life and growth. Blue is a reminder of heaven for all people: Even in cold northern countries the summer sky is blue. The Virgin Mary wears purple to emphasize her queenliness, or blue as a reminder of her heavenly home. The most expensive pigments were cinnabar red and ultramarine. Because they were rare, they were expensive; because they were expensive, they were associated with high status, whether human or divine. The Council of Ephesus in 431 established that Jesus had been God in the flesh from the moment of his conception when the Virgin Mary said yes to the angel's message. She was therefore not just the bearer of a human baby, but also the Mother or Bearer of God. The color of her clothes shows her status. The blue of the Mediterranean sky was appropriate for a picture of the Mother of God, the Queen of heaven.

So, contemplate the colors you see, as you pray through the icon before you.

PRAYER IS NOT SAFE BECAUSE GOD IS NOT SAFE

When you look at an icon prayerfully, that icon contains another person other than those in the picture—and that's you.

The Apostle John described what he saw in the Book of Revelation:

> . . . someone "like a "son of man," dressed in a robe reaching down to his feet and with a golden sash round his chest. His head and hair were white like wool, as white as snow, and his eyes were like blazing fire. His feet were like bronze glowing in a furnace, and his voice was like the sound of rushing waters. In his right hand he held seven stars, and out of his mouth came a sharp double-edged sword. His face was like the sun shining in all its brilliance. When I saw him, I fell at his feet as though dead. (Rev. 1:13–17)

The man who wrote those words had come face-to-face with the blinding glory of the risen and ascended Christ: he speaks of what he had seen and heard. In icons we see some of these words given an image, a physical meaning. When we come to icons in prayer, we are approaching this God and not anyone less: a sense of awe in entering his presence is an excellent beginning. "It is a dreadful thing to fall into the hands of the Living God" (Heb. 10:31). Yes, God is our loving Father, but also a God of awful majesty, before whom even the angels veil their faces. In Christ, we can approach him with confidence, but never with familiarity. "God is not a pussy-cat," Archbishop Anthony Bloom warns us.

Praying with icons opens up windows of relationship. It is a relationship so rich that we need to bring all of ourselves to it: it will involve heart and mind, eyes and ears, speech and silence and movement, our own words and the words of others; there will be exploration and evaluation, discovery, and delight.

PRAYING WITH A FEARFUL LOVE

Fear and love seem like opposite ends of a line, but in prayer that line becomes a circle. Begin where you are, travel in either direction, and you will come to the other side. Fear and love, love and fear, are like the wheels whirling within wheels that Ezekiel saw (Ezek. 1:15–28). To love what is greater than ourselves should be a fearful experience if we have a proper sense of proportion. Some people have ridiculed Western medieval artists for portraying God as a bearded old man, but are we any better in imagining the Creator of the universe as a benevolent Daddy at our beck and call? The prophets and apostles and the makers of icons would weep and howl at such presumption. We may become so busy being friendly with God that we forget who he is— and that would be dangerous.

Byzantine craftsmen pictured Christ as the Ancient of Days, and depictions of the Last

Judgment show him with the abode of the eternally blessed on his right hand and everlasting hell on his left. Worship was not presented as an easy activity, and there was no attempt at making it fun. One look at the *Christ Pantocrator* and you fell to the ground with *adoration*, a word that suggests fearful love. The greatest icons of Christ hold together the apparently antithetical qualities of justice and mercy. They are never harshly formidable, but neither are they ever sentimental.

A Window to God

Historically and theologically, the West has erred in visualizing God as a bearded old man sitting on a cloud. Neither Jews nor Eastern Orthodox Christians tried to make a picture of God the Father himself. It was forbidden. St. John tells us that no one has seen God at any time, but he (Christ), who dwells in the bosom of the Father, has revealed him (John 1:18). If we ask an Orthodox, "What does God look like?" he shows us the icon of Christ. God Incarnate, Jesus Christ, could be pictured in divine humanity, and the Holy Spirit could be shown in symbol by a dove or by tongues of fire. The Trinity could only be depicted in symbolic prefiguration as the three angels entertained by Abraham at Mamre (Genesis 18).

But to look into icons is to find a window to God. It is to look at God, to learn of God without seeing a picture of God the Father, but observing something about the nature of God or faith or sanctity. To look at God means simply "to look": I cannot explain it any other way. Give your attention to him and let your soul smile. I know that may sound fanciful and what some people would derisively call "a bit mystical," but it is something that must be done if prayer is ever to be more than either recitation or chatter. So do not analyze what it means to look at God: just do it. The facility has been built into you by the God who created you.

Do not think, though, that you must speak God's name in order to get his attention: he is already nearer to you than the air you are breathing. In any case, the names you address him by will vary from day to day, depending on how you are to him and on how he is to you. Often a loving look will be enough.

If these loving looks, the glancing prayers, are your only way for the next part of your pilgrimage into prayer, you will be moving forward. The pace may seem ludicrously slow compared with that of saints, but if you play the comparisons game, you will lose. You can meet God where you are now, wherever that may be, by looking. As you spend prayerful time with an icon, look at and be looked at by the great God, Who in Trinity is worshiped and glorified, and Whom we declare to be now set forth as clearly before you as the chains of our flesh allow, in

Jesus Christ our Lord, to Whom be glory for ever. Amen. (St. Gregory of Nazianzus, fourth century)

For Christians, for whom Christ is the living, incarnate image *par excellence* of the invisible God, surely the best and first choice of images before which to pray must be the icon of Christ, in whom "the whole fullness of God came to dwell bodily."

TAKE AT LEAST FIVE MINUTES

The way to begin with prayer is the way one begins to look at icons: slowly. I advise five minutes. That may feel short, but it is better to get a short time established than to begin with a longer one that you give up later.

Consider going into a church that has icons, so that the atmosphere is attentive to prayer. Some churches are open during the week, so anyone can go in to be quiet, look quietly, pray. Concentrate on developing the prayer of looking during these short times, and as the shape of your life changes, you can go on to a more sustained and focused time.

In icons, everyone will find rest for the soul. They have a good deal to tell us westerners; and they can arouse in us a holy orientation toward the supernatural. (Review of Ouspensky and Lossky in *La penseé catholique*)

When you have set yourself a time to be still before icons and to pray, and have kept to it, you will begin to discover a sense of order. You will find that the pattern of the day has brought with it an element of expectancy.

Train yourself to stick with five minutes a day for several months, and then extend the time to only ten minutes for several more months. There is no hurry. In the Western world today, and in countries influenced by the West, we live in an atmosphere of such speed and pressure that it is always safe to tell ourselves to go more slowly than we feel we should. Extend your time to fifteen minutes or longer only when you are sure you can use the time fully.

None of your prayer should be committed to paper, because this technique is a way of praying with the living flow of your thoughts, an image of an icon. Take it slowly and you will find that a rhythm is set up. Spontaneity and repetition balance each other, while the flow of thought is like the rhythm of breathing.

We can bring the prayers of the ages to our stillness before an icon. Here is a simple prayer from a Book of Hours, one of the books of private devotions used by the aristocratic laity in the late Middle Ages. The date of this one is 1514:

God be in my heart, and in my understanding;
God be in my eyes, and in my looking;

God be in my mouth, and in my speaking;
God be in my heart, and in my thinking;
God be at my end, and at my departing.

In times of great emotion, people return to the forms of prayer that they know best. A form the Jewish Christians would have known in addition to some of the psalms was the Eighteen Benedictions. Enrich yourself with such strong phrases from that ancient prayer as, "Heal us, O Lord, and we shall be healed. . . . Save us, and we shall be saved. . . ."

Follow the pattern with your own thoughts and needs, "Encourage me, O Lord, and I shall be encouraged. . . . Humble me, and I shall be humbled. . . ." Establish a verbal pattern and let your prayers flow within it.

Here is another prayer from the Eastern Orthodox Church; it is a threefold invocation called the *Trisagion*:

Holy God,
Holy and strong,
Holy and immortal,
    Have mercy upon us.

PRAYING WITHOUT WORDS

Don't be afraid of using your senses in prayer, in responding to something material.

C. S. Lewis wrote, "God likes matter, he invented it." In those six words he summed up the theology of the Creation and the Incarnation. Christianity is an incarnational religion, and icons focus on that theological center via a visual focus.

There is an inescapable physicality in Christian prayer and worship; it involves unspoken words formed in the mind by a complex process that not even neurologists claim to understand; worship involves words spoken with the tongue and the larynx; music produced by controlled breath, and instruments that make sound; limbs that walk, dance, sit, kneel, bow, prostrate, and trace the shape of the cross; taste buds that receive the dissolving texture of the Eucharist; eyes that notice the visual truth of an icon; ears that hear; noses that smell fresh flowers and (in some churches) incense and beeswax candles.

Consider that all wood and metal are special now because the Cross was made of wood and nails, that all water is special now because Christ was baptized in it, that all the ground is special now because he walked on it, and so on with every physical part of the world we live in. Rather than being evil, the material world, which includes our senses, is part of what our good God has made. Although it had been wrenched by the Fall, like a limb out of joint, the Incarnation took place in it and has changed it forever.

USE YOUR SENSE OF SIGHT

Sight has been used in godly worship from the beginning. The Old Testament is filled with pictorial object lessons: the garments of skin made by God for Adam and Eve, the lamb offered by Abel, the Temple adorned with sculpture, metalwork, spinning, dyeing, and weaving. The sense of sight has been used in Christian worship from the start, from a simple third-century picture of the Virgin and Child with a star in the Roman catacombs, to the windows of Chartres Cathedral ablaze with light, and on to some of the better examples of visual art in modern Churches.

Medieval Christians valued sight as the highest of the senses because it is connected with light, and God is light; that is why they brought light into their places of worship, filtering it through glass pictures that showed his glory. Before Gothic architecture with walls of light-transmitting glass, churches had the iconostasis and frescoed walls that were bright with pictures. Worshipers saw the Old Testament prophets, guardian angels, and events from the Gospels; every time they went into their Church they watched saints and sinners being divided as sheep from goats at the Last Judgment. They saw icons of Christ and his Mother and of their favorite saints. Those pictures stayed in their minds and hearts to correct, to guide, to warn, and to inspire.

FOUR

Some of the Most Recognizable Icons

RUBLEV'S *TRINITY* ICON

The finest picture of the Holy Trinity is St. Andrei Rublev's icon of Abraham's three visitors, an event interpreted by theologians as an Old Testament prophetic adumbration of Father, Son, and Holy Spirit. In Rublev's icon the three figures are not differentiated by a cruciform halo or by different ages.

It is possible to read them from left to right as Father, Son, and Holy Spirit. The figure on the left wears a robe of luminous colors, seeming to have been made of light; the central figure has a tunic with a broad stripe running down it, as seen in other pictures of Christ; the figure on the right of the panel has a mantle that is green. The central figure points a hand of blessing toward the chalice on the altar-table: we could therefore see the central figure as Christ, the great High Priest. By a subtle tilting of the heads, the left and central figures relate to each other while the figure on the right looks toward the chalice.

The identification of the three figures as (left-to-right) Father, Son, and Holy Spirit is not necessarily the only possibility, for when we consider the Trinity, we contemplate *one* God in tri-*unity*. St. Gregory Nazianzen writes that the three persons are distinguished only by *relationship* (not function, in which all three cooperate). The artist is trying to communicate the mystery of three persons, one in essence, power, and glory. In the end, speculation on which Person is which in the icon is pointless. It is notable that the three angels are identical in personal appearance—probably to counteract the possible misinterpretation of the icon as *tritheistic* (proposing three separate gods). However, it must be remembered that this is not a "portrait" of the ineffable Trinity, but a symbolic Old Testament "type" or prefiguration of the Christian mystery.

The landscape details are slight: a house indicates the place where Abraham and Sarah live, a tree indicates the oak of Mamre mentioned in Genesis 18. Light flows through the figures' clothes as though through shifting layers of fine silk. The three supernatural figures are represented by three angels, filled with beauty and strength and divine youth, relating to one another in an eternal song. The icon expresses both song and silence.

Of significance is the "circularity" of the composition: the three angels' forms and glances create a dynamic circle suggesting the eternal interchange of life and love within the eternal existence of the Trinity.

GOD THE FATHER

There are no icons of God the Father because of Exodus 33:20, which reads, "you cannot see my face, for no one may see me and live," and John 1:18: "No one has ever seen God; the only Son, who is in the bosom of the Father, he has made him known" (RSV). If you want to see the face of God, look at an icon of Christ.

God the Father, according to both the Old and New Testaments, cannot be seen by human eyes. He remains transcendent and has never manifested himself visibly to human sight. Since he is invisible, he cannot be depicted in an icon. The Greek Fathers insist that all the "theophonics" (manifestations of God) in the Old Testament were disclosures of the preincarnate Christ, the eternal Word and Wisdom of God, who is the exclusive and sole revealer of the Father. This is why in images of the Creation or of prophetic visions (Ezekiel, Daniel, etc.), it is Christ who manifests God or is shown in the act of creating. So when humans meet God, they behold the face of Jesus Christ.

The three Persons of the Trinity are not three gods. And because God is one, each Person of the Trinity manifests the other, so that an icon of Christ implies an icon of the whole Trinity.

GOD THE SON

The earliest pictures of Christ show him as youthful, elegant, and clean-shaven like the Roman gods Apollo or Mithras. In the Middle Ages, icons still sometimes show him as the youthful *Christ Emmanuel* (the name means "God with us"), especially when the accent is on his preexistence as eternal Son. In the fifth century the bearded face became standard and has continued to be the principal way he is shown. There is a cross in his halo so you can immediately distinguish Christ from the Apostles. His hand is in a position of blessing, commanding, or teaching. In some icons of the *Virgin and Child,* he is a miniature adult (though beardless), to show he had a knowledge and an identity beyond that of an ordinary purely human baby. This is precisely because he is the Incarnate Word and Wisdom of God. The Christ Child in icons usually holds a scroll to show he is God's Wisdom.

Icon craftsmen were not concerned with making a pretty picture of any mother and baby and then merely adding haloes. To paint him as an ordinary baby would be to say, visually, that he *was* an ordinary baby. Instead, the Byzantine craftsman was making a picture of the doctrine of the Incarnation.

GOD THE HOLY SPIRIT

In icons of the *Baptism of Christ*, the Holy Spirit is shown as a dove coming down on Christ's head, a reference to John 1:32. In Orthodox tradition, the Baptism is given much more weight than in the West, because it is seen as the first simultaneous disclosure of all three Persons of the Trinity in time: the Father's voice is heard (as later at the Transfiguration), the Spirit visibly descends in the form of a dove, and Christ is designated as Divine Son. This is why the Greek Fathers often call the Feast of the Baptism of Jesus Christ "the Theophany"—in other words, the Manifestation of the Triune God.

In icons of *Pentecost*, the Holy Spirit is shown as twelve rays of power or tongues of flame, one on the head of each Apostle. In icons of the *Annunciation* he (not "it") is coming down to the Virgin Mary as a tiny dove. She asked the Archangel about the conception of the Messiah (Luke 1:34–35): "How will this be . . . since I am a virgin?" The angel answered, "The Holy Spirit will come upon you, and the power of the Most High will overshadow you." In the icon, we see it happening.

The shaft of power is sometimes divided into three points to show that the whole Trinity is at work. Where the points join there is a circle, which may have a small white dove inside if the picture is big enough.

CHRIST PANTOCRATOR

Christ Pantocrator (pan-to-*cray*-tor) means Christ, the ruler of all.

The domed roof of a Byzantine Church represents the vault of heaven, and originally, mosaicists may have decorated it with the Ascension. By the tenth century, the figure in Church domes was half-length, and the picture for a dome had changed from narrative to confrontational. It was discovered that a half-length figure fitted more easily into a circle than one of full length, and it allowed the face to be on a larger scale. The most powerful image of *Christ Pantocrator* is at Daphni, near Athens, the mosaic made about 1100. He holds a closed book, which may be seen as the Gospels or as the Book of Judgment in Revelation 20:11, 12:

> Then I saw a great white throne and him who was seated on it. . . . Another book was opened, which is the book of life. The dead were judged according to what they had done as recorded in the books.

The fingers of his right hand are bent in the position of a priest's hand of blessing and are pointing toward himself. The index finger of his other hand points powerfully across the picture, balancing the sideways glance of his eyes to his left. When we look carefully at the face of this

Pantocrator, we see a difference between one side and the other. His right side, the side of blessing, is calm; his left side, the side of judgment, is fierce with an angry eyebrow. After nearly nine hundred years this awe-inspiring image still has the power to convert. Confronted with it for the first time some people react with shock: this is not a tame Jesus. The only thing that lets us off the hook is that those eyes do not look directly at us. The image is a reminder that the Last Judgment should be feared because it will be absolutely just, albeit tempered by mercy and total understanding.

The Pantocrator is not intended to represent Christ as the Jesus of Galilee, but as the awe-inspiring God-Man, the King of the Universe and terrible Judge at the end of time. By the fourteenth century, the severity of the terrible Judge is tempered, and in icons, a merciful Redeemer holds out his book with the text "I am the light of the world" (John 8:12), or "Come to me, all you who are weary and burdened" (Matt. 11:28).

THE HOLY FACE

The *Mandylion* (man-*dee*-lee-on), literally a napkin or handkerchief, is an icon of the face of Christ. According to the tradition of the Western Church, Veronica, a member of the crowd following Christ when he carried the cross, pressed her veil to his perspiring face; the cloth held the image, the details, of Christ's face on it.

In the Orthodox tradition, there is a different version of the story. King Abgar of Edessa sent a message to Christ to come and heal him, but Christ could not come. Instead he pressed a cloth to his face, thus miraculously imprinting his image on it, and sent it to the King who was healed by the sight of his face. The outlines of the face remained on the cloth as the "image not made with hands," and all the other icons of the *Holy Face* are claimed to have been copied from that prototype.

In AD 525 some workmen repairing the city wall of Edessa found a container with a cloth that had a face painted on it. It was called the image not made with hands, and was said to have been hidden in the wall by Christians when they had been persecuted. In the dry climate of Turkey a piece of linen could have been preserved for five hundred years. The cloth was taken to Constantinople in 944 and seems to have disappeared during the fourth Crusade, when the Latins sacked the city in 1204.

Why, in iconography, paint Christ's portrait as though on a cloth? Because tradition has it that the original cloth had been in contact with the holy face. No other icon portrait is painted as though it is on a cloth. For the Orthodox, the special significance of this icon lies in its miraculous production by Christ himself, thereby validating the practice of making icons.

The figure of the *Holy Face* is a man of about thirty, who looks straight at us with a calm expression. he has a cruciform halo with its identifying inscription. The face floats on a piece of white fabric like linen, painted either as though lying on the panel or hung by the top corners; sometimes it has a fringe across the lower edge. A difference between this portrait and other portraits is that this image has no neck (as though it is, indeed, an image taken from a cloth pressed to a person's face that maintains the image of the face, unlike a portrait, which contains a face, neck, and shoulders). The face we see is masculine and gentle. His dark brown hair is smooth on either side of his brow, and his short beard is pointed or forked. His hair descends in two locks. Orthodox tradition maintains that, here, one can see an authentic portrait of Jesus Christ.

THE ORDERS OF ANGELS
ARCHANGELS

The archangels most often seen in icons are Michael and Gabriel. Two others not often seen are Raphael and Uriel (mentioned in the book of Tobit and in the Jewish apocryphal Book of Enoch). They are shown in formal robes, in imperial dress, as God's *Vicegerents* (appointed deputies). They have wings and classical heads. Gabriel, the messenger of the *Annunciation*, carries a staff. Michael, protector of God's people, is often shown standing above a dragon, piercing him with his sword, a reference to Satan in Revelation 20:1, 2.

> I saw an angel come down out of heaven, having the key to the Abyss and holding in his hand a great chain. He seized the dragon, that ancient serpent, who is the Devil, or Satan, and bound him for a thousand years.

Many believe that at Armageddon, the final battle of good and evil, Michael will finally defeat and slay the dragon.

Icons of the archangel Michael (and of the assembly of the archangels) show him carrying a circular picture of Christ, an icon in an icon. In other icons he has an inscribed orb. (The inscription reads, "Jesus Christ, the just judge": overtones of Michael's role as weigher of souls at the Last Judgment.) Gabriel, too, can be depicted outside of narrative contexts, sometimes alone, more often paired with Michael in the *Deisis*.

Although St. Dionysius the Areopagite hierarchically distinguished nine orders of angels (the purely contemplative seraphim and cherubim coming first, or highest, and the ministering, active archangels and angels last), in practice the archangels are given preeminence, as God's viceroys here below, and as "taxiarchs" (commanders of the heavenly ranks of angels). Other categories of angels (some mentioned by St. Paul, for example, principalities and powers) are basically ignored

by the iconographic tradition (though they are
common in Western late medieval art).

CHERUBIM AND SERAPHIM

These two orders of angels, combined in one
rank, are described in the Old Testament:

> The sound of the wings of the cherubim
> could be heard as far away as the outer court,
> like the voice of God Almighty when he speaks.
> (Ezekiel 10:5)

> I saw the LORD seated on a throne, high
> and exalted, and the train of his robe filled the
> temple. Above him were seraphs, each with six
> wings: With two wings they covered their faces,
> with two they covered their feet, and with two
> they were flying. (Isaiah 6:1–2)

Seraphim in icons are often painted red as in the
fiery wheels-within-wheels in Ezekiel's vision. They
have shadowy or fiery faces half visible through the
feathers. They appear in icons of *Christ Pantocrator*
and the *Death of the Virgin* and elsewhere. In some
icons a single angelic figure painted red like fire
represents Christ, the wisdom of God, *Sophia*.

MORE ABOUT ANGELS

Angel means messenger. Angels are messengers
of God and guardians of the faithful. When angels
appear in the Old or New Testament, they are
described as young men in white robes; therefore,

following Biblical precedent it is proper to refer to an angel as "he." In icons they are young, male, beardless, and they often wear the white robes still seen in Christmas cards and Church windows. They are eternal youths, ageless but also sexless, like the eunuch-chamberlains of the Byzantine court. In an icon the robes appear in whatever color balances the other colors of the picture. Angels in icons also wear court dress or military costume, for angel courtiers are part of the early practice of using the splendors of the imperial court as an administration of the court of heaven. Military angels are the embattled guardians of the Christian people, actively engaged against Satan's cohorts.

Though angels in the Bible are not described as having wings, those in icons derive from the winged Victories or *genii* of Roman art. They look like winged Victories because such figures were part of the classical visual language known to the craftsmen and their patrons in the early centuries of the Church. Thus the visual formula of angels-with-wings-and-haloes is still understood today. Ask any child in Sunday school (or out of it) to draw an angel, and you can be sure the figure will have wings and probably a halo.

The iconography is simple and the iconography still works. The wings make the figures immediately identifiable, and since an icon is art for communication, it is important to know at whom you are looking. In an age when the fastest way for a person to travel was on a horse, people observed that creatures with wings, such as a hungry falcon or an eagle in a power dive, could travel even faster. As God's messengers, angels had wings to show them to be swift and airy travelers between heaven and earth. Angels have haloes because they are holy creatures carrying divine authority.

Because of their origins in pre-Christian Roman art, angels remain the most persistently classical figures in Byzantine art: They retain classical robes and coiffures, bound with a fillet, or often fully modeled, even in periods of more abstract style. They can even appear quite "beefy" and masculine (especially in works of the so-called fourteenth-century Macedonian School)—strange, one might think, when tradition insists that their forms are entirely ethereal (like fire), and the Byzantine liturgy calls them "holy bodiless powers of heaven"!

THE VIRGIN MARY

In the art of the Orthodox Church the Virgin Mary is usually shown with Christ because her status and importance are derived from him.

Icons of the Virgin Mary are in several iconographic types that are known by name. The differences between them are specific and of more significance than between Western Madonnas, which may differ only in styles of dress. In Orthodox Christian art, an icon of the Virgin presents to us a particular aspect of her life and significance.

An icon type of the Virgin Mary may be referred to by the name of a town, as in the Western Church we speak of Our Lady of Lourdes or of Walsingham. For example, the *Virgin Pelagonitissa* is an icon from Pelagonia, and the *Virgin of Vladimir* is so named because the icon was in that town for over two hundred years. Virgin icons with the reputation of being wonder-working are also often named after their towns of origin or residence, (e.g., the Virgin of Smolensk, of Tikhvin). Madonnas painted and sculpted in the West are sometimes crowned; Byzantine Virgins are crowned only in instances of Western influence.

Ways of depicting the Virgin Mary have developed over the centuries, from a stately Roman matron, to an equally stately Byzantine princess, or a richly dressed aristocratic lady, to a grieving and compassionate mother. In general, before the Age of Iconoclasm she was a theological figure, a visual presentation of the doctrine of the Incarnation. During those early centuries, the Church defined the doctrine of the Incarnation against heretical points of view: that Jesus Christ was not a God who dropped from the sky; that he was not a mere man who came to believe he was God; that he was not just a nice man who said wise things and whose followers exaggerated and fantasized. Rather, he was a single person, wholly God and wholly man, the Second Person of the Trinity Incarnate.

In the fifth century, Cyril of Alexandria wrote to Nestorius, Patriarch of Constantinople, to correct him on that completeness of incarnation:

> We do not say that first an ordinary man was born of the Holy Virgin and then the Word descended upon him, but we say that having the flesh, he accepted a carnal birth, because he claims this carnal birth as his own . . . so the Holy Fathers did not hesitate to call the Holy Virgin "Mother of God."

Whatever the type of icon, she always has the abbreviated inscription in Greek or Cyrillic letters to identify her as the Mother (or, the Bearer) of God. Iconography of the Virgin developed over generations as the Church grew in understanding of her.

Here are nine types of Virgin, and Virgin and Child icons, in roughly historical order.

VIRGIN ORANS

The *Virgin Orans* (*oar*-anz), the *Virgin Praying*, is the earliest type. Unlike most Eastern Church pictures of the Virgin, she is shown on her own, though an *Orans* icon may be only part of a group of praying figures. Even if Christ appears absent, he is present by implication as the One to whom the Virgin prays. In this type of icon we see the Virgin as intercessor and an example of the Church at prayer. She stands facing us with both hands raised level with her shoulders. Sometimes, for compositional reasons or lack of space, her hands are held up in front of her so her figure is a simple pillar and her hands are clearly visible against her dark clothes.

VIRGIN PLATYTERA

The *Virgin Platytera* (plat-tee-*tare*-ah) is also called the *Virgin of the Sign*. This type has been made since the Early Byzantine period.

The unborn Christ is in a roundel against the Virgin's breast, as an icon in an icon. Medievals did not believe that when a fetus was formed it was in the chest cavity. But a *Virgin of the Sign* icon is not an anatomically incorrect description of pregnancy; it shows that the Virgin Mary is the vehicle of the Incarnation. King Solomon prayed at the dedication of the Temple: ". . . will God dwell indeed with man on the earth? Behold, the heaven and the highest heaven cannot contain thee; how much less this house which I have built!" (2 Chron. 6:18 RSV). Mary is the living house of God that by grace can contain the uncontainable Divinity; poetically, therefore, her womb is said to have become "wider (*playtera*) than the heavens." It is a way of showing the miracle of the Incarnation (cf. John Donne: "Immensity encloister'd in thy dear womb"). In the *Theotokos'* pregnancy (*Theotokos* means "God-bearer") she became the Ark of the Covenant because God dwelt in her just as he was present in the Old Testament Holy of Holies. Since the human fetus that she carried was the Creator of all things, the womb that held him was "wider than the heavens."

The seventh-century Byzantine Akathist hymn referred to the mysterious fact:

> Hail, pure Mother of God, the Holy One of Israel.
>
> Hail, Thou whose womb is broader than the heavens.
>
> Hail, O sanctified one, O Throne of the heavens,
>
> Which the Children praised, saying:
>
> Bless ye the works of the Lord.

VIRGIN PARACLESIS

Paraclesis (par-*ra*-clee-sis) means the intercessor. Here, the Virgin is standing at three-quarters to the picture plane and turning toward Christ, who appears in a quadrant representing part of the arc of heaven at the top of the picture. Her elbows are close to her body and her hands spread toward him with the palms up in a gesture of prayer. In one hand she may hold an unfurled scroll with a list of prayer requests.

VIRGIN ENTHRONED

Mother and Child face directly toward us, as strong as a statue. As she is enthroned on the piece of furniture, so the child is enthroned on her lap. She presents the Child as directly as the Church presents him to us, and we should allow ourselves to read the figure as representing the Queen of heaven as well as the historical Mary of Galilee (not one or the other, but both-and). The frontality and direct gaze is similar to the *Orans* standing figure. The *Virgin Enthroned* is an iconic type that dates from the Early Byzantine period when the Virgin Mary was shown as a powerful Roman empress.

VIRGIN HODEGITRIA

The *Virgin Hodegitria* (ho-dee-*gee*-tree-ah) is a type that has been painted since the fifth century and was given its iconographic-name by the ninth century. The figures are usually half-length, and Mary has Jesus in the crook of her left arm. He is shown as a small adult rather than a child; he holds a scroll and extends his hand in blessing. She looks directly at us, extending the fingers of her right hand toward him. To understand icons, look first at the faces and the hands. It is the face and the hand that makes a Virgin icon a *Hodegitria* type: she looks at us and points our attention to him, and he, too, looks at us, so that we can meet him face-to-face.

Hodegitria means "The one who shows the way." (The *hodegoi* were guides who led blind pilgrims to a miraculous spring near Constantinople.) In a *Hodegitria* icon, the Virgin is a guide who directs our attention away from herself; it is the iconic representation of her words at the wedding in Cana, "Do whatever he tells you" (John 2:5). A

Hodegitria icon teaches the Incarnation, pointing emphatically to the authority of Christ.

There is a tradition that the original *Hodegitria* icon was painted by St. Luke who sent it to Theophilus with his Gospel.

VIRGIN ELEOUSA

The *Virgin Eleousa* (ell-e-*oo*-sa) is the Virgin of tenderness or compassion or loving-kindness. The most famous *Virgin Eleousa* icon is the twelfth-century *Virgin of Vladimir*, though the type was known before that date. It is a half-length icon with the Virgin and Christ cheek to cheek, his hand curling around her neck. Her head is turned so she looks at us with sorrow and compassion. Other tenderness icons show him reaching up to her face or caressing her veil.

The softer, embracing Mother was especially popular as a domestic icon, in contrast to the strong doctrinal images of the *Theotokos* made for the apse of a Church. The gentler image humanized Christ and the *Theotokos* as loving Mother and Son, while still asserting the doctrine of the Incarnation in visual form. In retrospect, we can see it was a large step toward painting Mary and Jesus as an ordinary mother and baby, in terms of universal human experience and feeling. It is of a piece with a shift in the late twelfth century in the way people were shown in Eastern Christian art: emotions were expressed outwardly, gestures were more dramatic. Even the clothes express emotion, fluttering with intensity as though the wearer's feelings have extended to the fabric.

VIRGIN OF THE BURNING BUSH

The burning bush that Moses saw, burning but not consumed, was later interpreted as a symbol of the Virgin Mary because she held the Light of the world, the fire of divinity, in her womb but was not consumed by his glory. In a *Burning Bush* icon, the Virgin and Child appear in a fiery bush; we are confronted by a frontal, full-length figure often accompanied by Moses, the recipient of the vision, and by other Old Testament prophets (see remarks above, on Christ as the subject of prophetic visions).

She holds Christ in front of her, his face directly below hers. He holds a scroll, and his right hand is raised in blessing. His knees are drawn up so it looks as though he is sitting on her forearm. In a *Burning Bush* icon, she presents him confidently to us.

VIRGIN OF THE PASSION

In ordinary speech today, the word "passion" refers to intense feelings of rage, enthusiasm, or sexual desire. In the context of religious art, the word means strong feelings that are deliberately endured. It is an active receiving of pain rather than a passive endurance of it. The passion of Jesus Christ is the pain of betrayal and crucifixion that he chose to go through even though, as he said, he could have called upon more than twelve legions of angels to rescue him (Matt. 26:53).

The *Virgin of the Passion* was a type that developed naturally from the *Virgin of Tenderness* in the late Middle Ages. The origin may have been Serbia in the fourteenth century, unless the tenth-century *Virgin and Child* in Tokali Kilise, Cappadocia, is an example. Because of the position of the child's limbs, icons of this type are sometimes wrongly called "Virgin with the Playing Child," but the Child is not playing. In the upper corners or sometimes on adjoining icons that have been lost, angels hold the instruments of the Passion. Mary can see the whip, nails, and cross; her brow creases in distress and her eyes shift sideways as she leans her head on the Child to protect him. The Child can see them, too; one of his little feet is turned up in tension as he writhes in his mother's arms. The icon invites consideration of Simeon's words to her: "a sword will pierce your own soul too. . ." (Luke 2:35). It questions how much the man who was God knew when he was a child. It points up the tragic inevitability of his salvific sufferings as an implication of the Incarnation.

PROTECTING VEIL OF THE MOTHER OF GOD (POKROV)

The *Virgin of the Veil* is a type that has been painted since the tenth century. She stands with her hands in prayer as angels fly above her holding a veil. St. Andrew the Holy Fool in the tenth century had a vision of the Virgin in the Church at Vlachernae, Constantinople. She was standing above them, praying and holding out her veil to protect Christians against invading Saracens.

Also present are the Imperial couple and St. Romanos the Melodist. This is originally, therefore, a record of a visionary experience, with profound religious political implications—not a discrete icon of the Virgin.

It became especially popular in Russia (*"pokrov"* literally means "tent" or "shelter" in Slavonic) when in the twelfth century, Prince Andrei Bogolinbski was the recipient of an almost identical vision: a holy fool saw the Virgin, attended by angels and apostles, in her cathedral at Vladimir, stretching out her veil to protect the Orthodox ruler and people from danger. It became the icon of the Virgin as national defender and intercessor for Holy Russia.

HOW TO RECOGNIZE OTHER POPULAR SAINTS

In the Eastern Orthodox Church a saint is identified as such more by physical characteristics than by what he or she is carrying. It is possible to recognize a saint simply by the head.

ST. JOHN THE BAPTIST

St. John the Baptist has unkempt brown hair and beard and an intense expression in his eyes, appropriate for a desert saint preaching, "Repent, for the kingdom of heaven is near." He is barefoot and is wearing a tunic made of camel skin or hair, as described in Mark 1:6. In some icons you can see the camel's head and legs still attached to the skin. His limbs are unnaturally thin. If not in a *Baptism of Christ* icon, he carries an unfurled scroll with the Marcan text quoted above. The prophet Elijah looks like the Baptist but much older, with the same intense expression. They seem to have been similar in personality, and the Baptist was called the second Elijah (Matt. 11:14).

St. John the Baptist is sometimes shown with wings. The logic of the craftsmen went like this: angels have wings (the Greek word *angelos* means messenger as well as angel [Mal. 3:1]), and the Baptist was the messenger of God's new covenant; therefore the Baptist may be painted with wings. The saint is also a paradigm of the ascetic life, considered an "angelic" life. A winged *St. John the Baptist* icon is a reminder that an icon maker shows spiritual realities rather than mere portraiture. John also frequently has his own severed head on a platter, a reference to his martyrdom at the hands of Herod.

THE APOSTLES PETER AND PAUL

The apostle Peter wears a blue tunic with a yellow cloak. He has curly gray hair brushed forward and a short full beard, round pink cheeks and a burly physique. He usually holds keys, a reference to Christ entrusting the keys of the kingdom to him (Matt. 16:19). (When an icon patron was from the Latin Church, he would instruct the craftsman to make St. Peter more prominent among the apostles than he might have been in Greek iconography.)

In icons, St. Paul is shown as a spare intellectual, holding a codex, more at home in a library than by the lakeside. His hair and medium-length, straggly beard are dark, and he is bald from the temples to the top of his head with tufts of hair showing further back.

The iconography of the two apostles (Paul and Peter) was established early because pilgrims to Rome wanted to take home pictures of them. A Roman medallion from the early fourth century shows what are already recognizable portraits. Here, St. Peter has a round head with curly hair and a full, curly beard. St. Paul has a high, domed forehead with receding, smooth hair and a ragged beard.

ST. GEORGE

St. George is a warrior saint and the patron saint of England (though he never came to England). In Early Byzantine icons, he is in Roman armor with a sword in his hand. He is young and beardless with a headful of rounded, springy curls and a clear-eyed, determined expression. Georgian icons of the ninth century show his horse trampling on the Emperor Diocletian, like Imperial figures on Roman coins trampling on shaggy-coated barbarians from Northern Europe. In later icons he is often on horseback killing a dragon with his lance, an epitome of the victory of good over evil.

For seven hundred years—a considerable stretch of history—he was St. George without the dragon, a soldier saint like Theodore or Demetrius. The earliest dragon-slaying picture is in a rock Church in Cappadocia, Turkey, painted in the late eleventh century.

Often, too, we see the saint rescuing a maiden from the hungry dragon, a legend told and retold since the sixth century. The story followed the mythic pattern of Perseus and Andromeda, and of all the hissing, scaly monsters of English folk tales from Helston to the Orkneys.

With St. Demetrius, St. George is the most popular of Orthodox military saints, considered a "great martyr" and protector of the faithful.

ST. NICHOLAS OF MYRA

The third-century bishop Nicholas is shown in icons with beard and gray hair, receding at the temples. The line of his short beard emphasizes his hollow cheeks, and he has a wrinkled forehead that makes him look worried. His face is pear-shaped with wide high forehead and narrow jaw. He wears an *omophorion* with black crosses on it to show that he is a bishop. He carries a codex, and his hand is raised in blessing. His expression is calm and direct, benign but sometimes with a touch of severity.

A *Life of St. Nicolas*, written in the fifth century, describes him as "meek and gentle in his disposition and humble in spirit." He is the patron saint of Russia, and also of children and students.

There are more extant icons of St. Nicholas than of any other saint except the Virgin—an indication of his huge popularity both in East and West.

AND LESS FAMILIAR FIGURES

To see unfamiliar saints is a reminder to Western Christians that there are many more specially dedicated holy men and women in the East than the ones recognized as saints by the Western Church. For instance there is St. Paraskeva (in Russian, *St. Piatnitsa*, meaning Friday). Since Friday was market day, she became the patron of stall holders who sell groceries and wares, and of women who buy them. Among the many others are Saints Cosmos and Damian, familiar in Tuscan art as patrons of the Medici. These are doctor saints, shown in icons with spatulas and medicine boxes. And there are countless more.

Many icon saints gaze directly at us, silently willing us to be strong. The Seventh Ecumenical

Council, 787, justified the use of icons in Christian devotion: "For each time that we see their representation in an image, we are made to remember the prototypes, we grow to love them more."

HERMITS, ABBOTS, MONKS, AND NUNS

Many icons celebrate those who have set themselves apart for the religious calling. Some were founders of monastic communities, some famous theologians or ascetics.

Men and women from all levels of society made a decision to step apart from the pleasures and pressures of Roman society to live in simplicity before God. Two of the first hermits recorded were St. Paul of Thebes and St. Anthony of Egypt, third century. St. Pachomius of Tabennisi organized a group of hermits into a common life with a daily rule of prayer and manual work, similar to the Rule of St. Benedict in the Western Church. The solitary and communal life combined in Palestine in the Lavra, in which monks lived in separate cells and met on Saturdays and Sundays.

The landscape of Byzantium was dotted with small monastic houses and hermit caves. In Cappadocia, entire churches were carved out of solid rock, complete with pillars, domed ceilings and blind windows. Icons of hermit saints show the men who chose to live in that rocky landscape; they were shown with emaciated arms and faces, reflecting their prolonged fasting and self-mortification.

The lives of some solitaries may seem extreme to us, but entirely reasonable to them. They survived mainly on pulses, bread, vegetables, and water. One lived in an iron cage till his feet froze to the floor. Some, called "Stylites" (e.g., St. Simeon, St. Daniel), escaped from the world vertically as well as inwardly, living on small platforms at the tops of pillars with every aspect of their lives open to the public gaze. Other hermits, called "dendrites," like David of Salonica, lived in tree houses. St. Neophytos made his home in a cave for more than fifty years. St. Mary of Egypt, a former prostitute, wandered in the desert dressed only in her hair; in icons she is as skinny as a cadaver, her hair flowing to her knees.

The hermits' steely commitment to Christ was something that has never been easy to comprehend. Icons of hermit saints are a challenge to Christians and to Western society. The figures face us calmly, some of them holding a scroll with words of exhortation or a Bible verse. They are emaciated and determined, magnificently out of step with society.

Perhaps because of their self-marginalized position, such hermits frequently exercised a prophetic witness in society, able to rebuke the powerful with impunity. People came to them to seek spiritual counsel and healing—but keep in mind that Orthodox monks are first and foremost contemplatives, not teachers or social workers.

An icon of a hermit saint invites salutary consideration of the relationship between sanity and holy folly, and of a vision of glory so vivid that it influences life in this world.

HOLY FOOLS

Holy Fools are a special category of solitaries and of ascetics, pictured in icons, especially in Russian icons. They are solitaries in the sense that they have separated themselves from ordinary society and are homeless, constantly wandering and living on alms. They lack proper clothes and invite scorn for the sake of religious calling, even feigning madness. This is perhaps the most radical form of ascetic self-stripping and radical dependence on God, going even further than the hermit in his cave, let alone the monks with their life of corporate stability and property. We recall that St. Paul was proud to call himself a "fool" for Christ's sake (1 Cor. 4:10).

SATAN AND HIS ANGELS

Because of the Orthodox Church belief that an icon is a privileged point of contact with the heavenly world, Satan and his angels are seldom shown. If they are, they appear in profile and in pictures of the *Last Judgment*. They also appear in the *Temptation of Christ* and other narrative New

Testament subjects in manuscripts, frescoes, and (rarely) icons.

In an eleventh-century icon of the *Ladder of Perfection* at Sinai, devils are preventing monks from ascending the ladder to heaven; their demonic armaments include hooks, and bows and arrows. In the Latin Church and sometimes in the Christian East, hell is shown as an enormous, lipped mouth like the mouth of a fish, opened wide to receive the damned. Satan's angels, in and around that mouth, are in violent, disorganized movement, as though held forever in clanking, chaotic noise. By contrast, God's angels and saints are in control and usually calm.

In an eleventh-century icon of the *Last Judgment*, Satan is sitting on a throne made of a seven-headed serpent, like the seven-headed beast in the Book of Revelation. Behind him is a wall of flames. He looks like an infernal version of Abraham, who sits on the opposite side of the picture, cradling the saved on his lap. The Devil has a lost soul (probably Dives, the rich man in Luke 16:19–31) on his knee and is welcoming other souls to that ultimate horror, a party to which no one wanted to go and that will never end.

FIVE

Final Thoughts

W E HAVE SEEN HOW SOME ICONS are statements of heavenly realities, such as *Christ Pantocrator*, or praying saints, while others depict historical events, especially key moments in the life of Christ that Christians believe are of permanent saving value to humanity. If we understand the "weight" an effective icon must bear as the focus of prayer and revealer of the divine, we will also understand the expressionistic conventions often used by their creators: the lack of shadows, the conscious distortions of form, the inversion or denial of perspective; similarly, the frontal, hieratic presentation of individual saints (or Christ alone) with the exaggerated staring eyes and pale features. The aim is to communicate the impinging of the divine world upon the human one.

The aim is to depict persons already in the process of deification or transfiguration, and to show history as the sphere of divine intervention— "the intersection of the timeless moment."

LIVING DOORS

In a mysterious way, the icon is believed to make present what it represents; it can communicate the presence and something of the spiritual nature of the holy person depicted (Christ, the Virgin, or some other saint). As such it is a means of grace, something approaching a sacrament. This is why the icon is an object of veneration: lights and incense are burned before it, people bow before it and kiss it.

Of course, the icon is not sacramental in the same sense as the Eucharist, which is not just an image of the Christ but is his true Body and Blood, something to be worshiped. Nonetheless, on a different level, Christ is also present in his icon. Its matter (the wood, paint, etc.) is a channel of spiritual grace, as is the water of baptism or the oil of chrismation.[2] St. Theodore the Studite writes, "We should believe that divine grace is present in the icon of Christ, and that it communicates sanctification to those who draw near with faith."[3]

The art of icons is not dead; icons are still being made and still being used in Christian worship. News stories from Russia or Eastern Europe sometimes give a glimpse of the Orthodox Liturgy. The images leave us with an impression of darkness and brightness, incense and candles, deep voices chanting, and icons. The pictures are not there just to be looked at as though the worshipers were in an art museum: they are designed to be doors between this world and another world, between people and the Incarnate God, his mother, or his friends, the saints.

If a door is to do its job, it must have throughput in two directions. As we move toward an icon, it moves toward us with a warm and precise Christian content—if we understand the language that it speaks. The primary purpose of an icon is to enable a face-to-face encounter with a holy person or make present a sacred event, but icons are also "theology in color."

An icon reflects the life, historical experience, and belief system of Eastern Christianity in all of its complexity and depth. As an integral part of that life, it aspires to offer a "window," a vision (however imperfect) of a transfigured world and humanity. This all points forward to the final revelation of glory in the age to come.[4]

NOTES

1 Thomas Howard, *Evangelical Is Not Enough: Worship of God in Liturgy and Sacrament* (Nashville: Thomas Nelson, 1984), 72.

2 Used both in confirmation (in Orthodoxy, part of baptismal initiation) and for the anointing of the sick and dying.

3 *Letter on the Cult of the Holy Images*, p. 100, 505B (so, decree of Nicaea II; Mansi *Concilia XIII*, 269E). "If the person depicted is full of grace, the material object (the icon) shares in that grace to an appropriate extent" (St. John of Damascus, *On Icons* I.36). Cf. The Nicene Creed: "When we honor and venerate an icon, we receive sanctification" (Mangi, *Concilia XIII*, 269 E).

4 For those wishing to read further about the theology of the icon, the best book for beginners is probably still Lossky-Ouspensky's *The Meaning of Icons* (1952), or Linette Martin's own larger work, *Sacred Doorways: A Beginner's Guide to Icons* (2002).

FOR FURTHER READING

Alpatov, M. *Color in Early Russian Icon Painting*. Moscow: Iskusstro, 1974.

———. *Early Russian Icon Painting*. Moscow: Iskusstro, 1978.

Baggley, J. *Doors of Perception: Icons and their Spiritual Significance*. London: Mowbrays, 1987.

Brenske, H. *Icons, Windows to Eternity*. Brussels: Berghous Verlag, 1990.

Chatzidakis, M. *Icons of Patmos*. Athens: National Bank of Greece, English edit., 1985.

Cormack, R. *Writing in Gold: Byzantine Society and its Icons*. London: George Philip, 1985.

Ouspensky, L. *Theology of the Icon*. New York: St. Vladimir's Press, 1978.

———, and V. Lossky. *The Meaning of Icons*. New York: St.Vladimir's Press, 1982.

Trubetskoi, E. N. *Icons: Theology in Color*. New York: St. Vladimir's Press, 1973.

ANCIENT SPIRITUAL DISCIPLINES

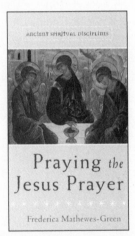

PRAYING THE JESUS PRAYER
Frederica Mathewes-Green

64 pages ISBN: 1-978-1-61261-059-7
$24.95 (pack of 5), Small paperback

Available from most booksellers or
through Paraclete Press